GREEN ANOLES AS PETS

Everything You Need to Know About Green Anole, the Facts, Care, Housing, Feeding and Behavior

Dr. Peters Joe

Table of Contents

CHAPTER 1

PROLOGUE OF GREEN ANOLE

Green anoles are recognized by means of numerous names anyway they might be furthermore known for their capacity to change tones from unpracticed to brown and lower back once more (in spite of the way that they are currently not appropriate chameleons). They are as often as possible discovered walking around and luxuriating in the sun inside the Southeastern United States and islands inside the Caribbean just as in terrariums over the use of an as pets.

• Name: Anolis carolinensis, unpracticed anole, Carolina anole, American anole, American chameleon, red-throated anole

• Size: Males accomplish 8 inches protracted, (for example, the tail) in imprisonment yet are bigger in the wild; females are littler

• Lifespan: Around 4 years, regardless of the way that they can satisfy eight or more prominent years, if pleasantly thought about

GREEN ANOLE BEHAVIOR AND TEMPERAMENT

Green anoles are the best variety of anole neighborhood to the United States; they can be found inside the wild in Tennessee, Louisiana, Georgia, Florida, the Carolinas, and Texas. Green anoles are well known and make great "starter" pets for kids. These very little reptiles have emerald-green backs and pink "dewlaps" (pockets underneath their jaws). An infrequent anole can likewise really have a blue color.

Anoles are amusing to watch, as they're vigorous all through the sunlight hours and like to climb. One in their top of the line credits is their ability to have cooperation with their human proprietors; many are happy to eat up from their proprietors' hands. While it is high-caliber to get an anole (and many appreciate roosting on a human shoulder), it's vital to avoid getting them by methods for the tail. Rather, train youths to choose them up with the guide of setting a hand under the reptile's gut.

PART 2

LODGING THE GREEN ANOLE

Anoles can be housed in a sensibly little tank or terrarium. A 10-gallon tank is sufficient for a solitary or pair of anoles. A bigger tank is, obviously, better in spite of the fact that and on the off chance that you are lodging numerous anoles masses of territory is fundamental.

You need to just keep one male anole as indicated by tank. Females will get along agreeable insofar as the tank is open adequate, and there a lot of lounging spots and two or three areas to cover up. A safely outfitted top is important since green anoles can crush through little places.

A dampness level of 60 to 70 rates is significant for unpracticed anoles (utilize a hygrometer to screen those levels). This can regularly be finished by moistening the internal of the tank every day. Clouding frameworks are to be had in spite of the fact that they're very costly. In the event that you are making some troublesome memories holding the dampness level take a stab at covering a piece of the highest point of the tank as well as developing the assortment of live plants in the nook. Clouding moreover gives expending water for the anoles as they regularly will now not drink from a bowl (they may lick beads of water off the moistened vegetation like chameleons).

During the day make sure to give a warm slope from seventy five to eighty F (24 to 27 C) with a lounging spot of eighty five to 90 F (29 to 32 C). A blend of under tank radiators and a lounging gentle on one part of the tank works pleasantly. Ensure the appropriate temperature angle is given through estimating temperatures in different spots around the tank. Night temperature can drop to an angle of sixty five to 75 F (18 to 24 C). Try not to utilize white lolling lighting installations to obtain evening temperatures anyway on the other hand use warming cushions, artistic warming components, or uncommon night heat lighting apparatuses.

Notwithstanding the radiant lounging light, you bring to the table a full range UVA/UVB light for 10 to 12 hours reliable with day. This extraordinary gentle will help spare you your anole from developing metabolic bone infection and keep up them looking brilliantly shaded, vigorous, and glad. The bulb wishes to be changed out every a half year (despite the fact that it hasn't wore out) and nothing ought to hinder the light other than a steel work screen (no plastic or glass).

SUBSTRATE

Substrate of peat greenery and soil with or without a layer of bark (e.G. Orchid bark) is a super substrate for anoles. Live vegetation help keep up moistness and offer spread. Most loved live blossoms comprise of sansevierias (snake vegetation), bromeliads, philodendrons, ivy, orchids, and vines. Bits of bark and branches should furthermore be outfitted for hiking and luxuriating. Maintain a strategic distance from sleek or scented substrates comprising of lumber shavings, and avoid dry substrates comprising of sand.

The supported substrates comprise of soil (without perlite), peat greenery, or orchid bark. Basically, a semi-tropical condition should be made (presently not downpour timberland) with daytime temperatures of 75 to eighty F and a mugginess of 70 percent.

PART 3

FOOD AND WATER

Green anoles are insectivores and are regularly acceptable eaters. While crickets can be the principle a piece of the food routine, its miles charming to take care of various gut stacked bugs including mealworms and wax worms. Feed two to 3 precisely measured prey contraptions which are about portion of the components of the anole's head each unique day. A calcium and diet supplement should moreover be tidied at the bugs. A few vegetation should be outfitted, and branches for lounging are fundamental. Anoles don't lap water from a dish when in doubt, so their confines/vegetation should be clouded multiple times every day. The anoles get their liquids by utilizing licking beads off of leaves.

Green anoles do pleasant on a ton of digestive tract stacked bugs which incorporate mealworms and wax worms. Feed a few precisely measured prey contraptions which can be about portion of the size of the anole's head each other day. A calcium and diet supplement should furthermore be cleaned at the bugs. Be cautious allowing your anole to get wild creepy crawlies; there's no way to perceive what sorts of pesticides wild-got bugs may convey.

REGULAR HEALTH PROBLEMS

In standard, green anoles are solid creatures and are once in a while sick. They can, in any case, create breathing issues, mouth decay, or a metabolic bone issue that impacts in weight reduction and swollen joints. Search for:

- Swollen joints

- Loss of craving

- Smelly or runny stool

- Weight misfortune

- Difficulty relaxing

- Discharge from nose, eyes or mouth

- Shedding issues or stained skin

you have to consistently look for exhortation from a veterinarian in the event that you see any of these issues. In the interim, notwithstanding, do test to be certain that your pet's substrate and weight reduction plan are fitting, as issues with these are as often as possible the explanation of stress-related disease.

PICKING YOUR GREEN ANOLE

Green anoles are accessible at practically any pet store and should be economical (under $20). Search for an enthusiastic, ready example and ensure that various anoles at the store look healthy and all around thought about. It's useful to realize that lacking toes aren't an issue: green anoles lose and recover them with no wellbeing suggestions.

Give your new pet a few days to adapt to its new residential before taking it out to play. In the event that conceivable, find a vet with reptile experience, and acquire your unpracticed anole for a "pleasantly pet" test.

Green anoles are ordinary and make an exact apprentice reptile. They have the advantage of being very little, cheap, and simple to think about. It is genuinely simple to satisfy their lodging and healthful prerequisites, in spite of the way that some particular device is expected to appropriately set up a vivarium for anoles for the essential time.

- Names: Anolis carolinensis, Green anole, Carolina anole, American anole, American chameleon, and red-throated anole

- Size: Males are around eight inches extensive (along with the tail) in bondage anyway are enormous inside nature. Females are littler than guys.

- Life Span: Average 4 years, anyway can remain up to eight years

PART 4

CONDUCT AND TEMPERAMENT OF GREEN ANOLES

Anoles can be spared alone or in little enterprises. Guys are regional and may likewise show and battle with each other, so an assortment is top notch made out of ladies with no two or three male.

These reptiles are some of the time called American chameleons, in spite of the way that they are presently not genuine chameleons. Anoles can trade their shading from earthy colored to splendid emerald unpracticed. The green anole is nearby toward the southeastern United States and the Caribbean.

Anoles are likewise engaging little reptiles. Guys have a vivid dewlap (the crease of skin underneath the jawline/neck), which they streak over the span of regional and romance showcases. Females of certain species additionally have dewlaps, despite the fact that they are commonly littler and not showed as often as possible.

They can drop their long tail as a protection against predators in nature. It's currently not a genuine idea to keep up them with the guide of the tail. At the point when an anole drops its tail, it will normally recover yet won't seem to be like the first. Green anoles are touchy and timid, however with consistent and delicate adapting to, they will end up being somewhat manageable.

LODGING GREEN ANOLES

Anoles might be put away by me or in little offices. Guys are regional and may likewise show and battle with each other, so a gathering is good made out of women without any than one male. A full-size aquarium with a tight-turning out to be screen top makes the incredible home; a flat out negligible 10-gallon aquarium for a couple, anyway bigger is higher and important for organizations of three or extra.

These reptiles are specifically diurnal (vigorous all through the daytime) and simultaneously as they want to relax as a great deal as the accompanying reptile, they decide to do as such among plants. They're dynamic little critters, who rush about rapidly, making them difficult to trap. They lean toward no longer to be dealt with too bounty; keep away from it assuming there is any chance of this happening, and consistently manage them delicately. Never dangle green anoles by utilizing the tail.

The cushions on the bottoms of their feet grant them to climb and stick to most surfaces and to escape fenced in areas that are not secure.

Green anoles are lovely enough pets, however their characteristic instinct is to safeguard their domain. Guys will attempt to uncover predominance by means of stretching out their dewlaps to appear to be bigger to planned mates. In the event that it opens and shuts its dewlap, this is a sign of animosity and markers that the creature is feeling hazardous or compromised.

PART 5

PICKING YOUR GREEN ANOLE

On the off chance that a hostage reproduced reptile can be procured, that is best, as they tend to be less bugged and substantially less helpless to disease or turmoil at the hour of procurement. Most anoles to be had in pet shops are wild gotten. Some of the time, pet keep anoles may be got dried out and starved when bought, as confirm through free creases of skin.

Maintain a strategic distance from anoles that look wiped out or got dried out. New anoles must be checked by means of a veterinarian for internal and outer parasites.

Despite the fact that anoles are entirely simple to think about, this doesn't generally make them a low-redesign pet. Recollect that reptiles are not surprising suppliers of Salmonella microorganisms, so legitimate cleanliness is important when managing them and cleaning their framework, particularly if children or individuals with debilitated insusceptible frameworks remain in a similar house.

NORMAL HEALTH PROBLEMS

In the same way as other reptiles, unpracticed anoles are vulnerable to an infirmity known as mouth decay or stomatitis. In the event that you note puffiness or redness round its mouth or a substance that appears as though curds round its teeth, it's more than likely mouth decay.

This circumstance requires cure by methods for a veterinarian with reptile skill. Try not to endeavor to treat this with a local cure; this agonizing condition can prompt teeth misfortune and at last contaminate the reptile's jaw. Mouth decay might be fatal whenever left untreated.

Metabolic bone disease, which originates from a poor eating routine or absence of UVB presentation, shows indications of weight decrease, puffy face, and general shaky area and torpidity. Redressing the weight-decrease plan and presenting your anole to a satisfactory measure of UVB beams should help.

Different reptiles are helpless against breath contaminations; anyway those are very abnormal in unpracticed anoles. They're not, at this point inconceivable, be that as it may. In the event that your anole is wheezing or saving its mouth open, those are indications of a breathing contamination, normally because of deficient mugginess or warmth in its nook.

On the off chance that your anole isn't continually turning unpracticed and seems, by all accounts, to be idiotic earthy colored shading, this can be a sign it's far compelled or shows a fundamental wellness issue.

THE END

www.ingramcontent.com/pod-product-compliance
Lightning Source LLC
Chambersburg PA
CBHW070327160726
47999CB00003B/1197